Mary McLeod Bethune's Many Achievements

Kate Broad

Boston, Massachusetts
Chandler, Arizona
Glenview, Illinois
Upper Saddle River, New Jersey

Illustrations
Opener, 1, 3, 4, 5, 7, 8, 9, 10 Bob Dacey.

Photographs
Every effort has been made to secure permission and provide appropriate credit for photographic material.
The publisher deeply regrets any omission and pledges to correct errors called to its attention in subsequent editions.

Unless otherwise acknowledged, all photographs are the property of Pearson Education, Inc.

Photo locators denoted as follows: Top (T), Center (C), Bottom (B), Left (L), Right (R), Background (Bkgd)

2 Library of Congress; 6 Library of Congress; 14 ©Andersen Ross/Blend Images/Getty Images; 15 Library of Congress.

ISBN-13: 978-0-328-67643-9
ISBN-10:   0-328-67643-8

5 6 7 8 9 10 V0FL 15 14 13

An Unjust System

Mary McLeod Bethune was the first child in her family to be born free. The Civil War had ended slavery. Yet African Americans were still not free in many ways. They lived under a system that kept them **segregated**, separate from whites. Bethune dedicated her life to helping African Americans overcome segregation.

Under segregation, African Americans could not attend the same schools, eat in the same restaurants, or shop in the same stores as white Americans. They had to ride in different railway cars. They could not even use the same water fountains.

They faced **discrimination**, unfair treatment because of their race, in other ways, too. African Americans could not get the same jobs as white Americans or live in the same neighborhoods. They did not have the same opportunities to improve their lives.

Separate but Not Equal

Schools for African American children were supposed to be equal to schools for white children. In reality, schools for African American children were not as good as schools for white children. Buildings were run-down, overcrowded, and lacked supplies. Books were old, torn, or not to be had at all. Teachers were poorly paid. In many places there were no schools for black children at all.

From the beginning, Mary McLeod Bethune knew education was key. Education could open doors for people. She wanted African Americans to have the opportunity for a good education.

The Birth of a Leader

Mary McLeod Bethune was born in Mayesville, South Carolina, on July 10th, 1875, to Patsy and Samuel McLeod. Mary McLeod's parents and her older brothers and sisters had lived as slaves before the Civil War. Mary McLeod was born after slavery ended.

The McLeod family worked hard and saved enough money to buy a farm of their own. They raised rice and cotton. Like the rest of her family, Mary McLeod worked in the fields. Even as a child, she was a hard worker. When she was nine, she could pick 250 pounds of cotton in a single day!

You Can't Read That!

Before slavery ended, it was against the law to teach enslaved people to read and write. So, no one in the McLeod family was **literate**.

Patsy McLeod often worked doing laundry for a white family named Wilson. Sometimes Mary McLeod went with her and played with the Wilson children. One day she picked up one of the children's books. She opened it, curious to see what was in it.

"You can't read that—put that down!" the Wilson girl demanded. Mary McLeod dropped the book and looked at a picture book the girl gave her instead, but the Wilson child's words stung her pride. She wanted to read, too.

Learning and Teaching

From that moment on, Mary McLeod was determined to learn to read. But there were no schools African American children could attend in Mayesville. Then a teacher came from another town to start a school for African American children. She asked the McLeods to send their children, but the family could only afford to send one child. Mary McLeod begged to go. Her parents allowed her to go. She was one of the first to enroll.

Mary McLeod had to walk five miles to the school and back, but she didn't complain. She studied hard, doing her homework by candlelight at night. Soon Mary McLeod was giving back, using her education to help others. She read letters for her neighbors who could not read for themselves. She read the Bible to the family. She even taught her older brother to read.

The school Mary McLeod attended may have looked like this one.

When Mary McLeod was about fourteen, a teacher in Colorado sent money for one student to attend Scotia Seminary in North Carolina. Again, Mary McLeod was chosen. Her neighbors, both black and white, helped supply her with the clothing and other necessities she would need to go. When she left on the train, all the neighbors came to the station to see her off. Mary McLeod did well at the school and made many friends among the teachers and students. Later, she studied religion at a school in Chicago.

Now Mary McLeod was a young woman. She knew what she wanted to do with her life: She wanted to help others learn. So after graduation, she moved back to South Carolina to be a teacher. There, she met and married a handsome former schoolteacher named Albertus Bethune. Albertus found a job in Georgia, so they moved, and Mary Bethune continued to teach.

Mary McLeod Bethune Starts a School

Bethune wanted to do more. She wanted to build a school where there was the greatest need—where there weren't any schools for African American students. She decided to go to Florida. She knew many African Americans were moving there.

In 1904, Bethune found an empty four-room house in Daytona Beach, Florida. She turned the rented house into a school for African American girls. She called it the Daytona Literary and Industrial Training School for Negro Girls.

Bethune's students were very busy. They learned reading, writing, and math. The girls also learned sewing, dressmaking, cooking, and how to grow their own food.

Today Bethune's school is a university with more than three thousand students.

In the beginning, it was a challenge to keep the school open. Bethune had only $1.50 and five students. There were no desks. Instead, the students sat on boxes. There were few supplies such as paper and pens. Bethune had the students make their own ink from elderberries. "Use what you have in your hands," she said.

Many wealthy northerners visited Daytona for the winter. Bethune didn't hesitate to go to their hotels to ask for help. She got it, and she also got help from people in the community who believed in the school. Her determination to succeed impressed businessmen and **philanthropists** such as James N. Gamble and John D. Rockefeller. They gave money, and the school began to grow. In two years, there were 250 students. In 1923, it combined with a boys' school called the Cookman Institute and became Bethune-Cookman College. Today it has more than three thousand students.

Working for Equal Rights

While she was improving her school, Bethune worked to help African Americans gain equality. One way she did this was to make sure that African Americans were able to vote in local elections.

There were several obstacles that prevented African Americans from voting. Many African Americans, as well as poor white people, were required to pay a tax, called a **poll tax**, before they could vote. Bethune raised money so African Americans could afford the tax.

In many places, African Americans had to pass a literacy test to show they knew how to read and write before they could vote. Bethune taught classes to help people prepare for the test.

Jim Crow Laws

The laws that kept African Americans from voting and segregated them from white Americans were known as Jim Crow laws. Jim Crow was not a real person, but the name of a character in a song.

The Jim Crow laws kept African Americans separated from whites in schools, restaurants, railroad cars, and dozens of other places. But Jim Crow was more than a set of laws. It also meant unwritten laws and customs. For example, African Americans had to call whites "Sir," "Mister," or "Ma'am." Whites called African Americans by their first names.

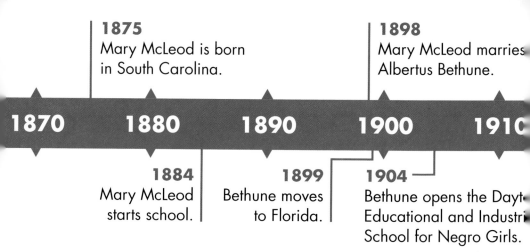

1875
Mary McLeod is born in South Carolina.

1898
Mary McLeod marries Albertus Bethune.

1870 **1880** **1890** **1900** **1910**

1884
Mary McLeod starts school.

1899
Bethune moves to Florida.

1904
Bethune opens the Dayt Educational and Industri School for Negro Girls.

The Right to Vote

Bethune also fought for the vote for women. Women in many states, both black and white, were not able to vote before 1920. But Bethune wanted all adult citizens to be able to vote and worked along with others to change the laws.

Not everyone wanted African Americans to vote. Some white citizens of Daytona Beach were members of the Ku Klux Klan, a secret organization that threatened and even killed African Americans to keep them from voting. These whites were angry with Bethune, too, and threatened her. But Bethune did not back down. With Bethune's help, more than one hundred African Americans voted in the next election.

| 1920 | 1930 | 1940 | 1950 | 1960 |

1920
Women gain
the right to vote.

1954
School
segregation ends.

1935
Bethune becomes
a special advisor to
President Roosevelt.

1955
Bethune dies in
Daytona Beach, Florida.

A Leader in Washington

As Bethune's school grew in reputation, so did Bethune's influence. Her work caught the interest of people in the nation's capital, too. She was even asked to be an advisor to Presidents Calvin Coolidge and Herbert Hoover.

In 1927, through her work with women's groups, Bethune met Eleanor Roosevelt, whose husband, Franklin Delano Roosevelt, was an important politician in New York. The two women began to work together on projects to help women, children, and African Americans. They soon became close friends. Later, when people criticized Bethune's ideas, Eleanor Roosevelt wrote letters defending her.

When Franklin Delano Roosevelt became president in 1932, he made Bethune a special advisor. Bethune gave the president suggestions on how to fight discrimination. She shared ideas about how to encourage races to work together.

Changes for America

In 1954, the United States Supreme Court made a historic decision. It decided that school segregation was against the Constitution. It was now against the law to have separate schools for African American and white students. Now black and white students would have the same opportunities to go to school.

Mary McLeod Bethune died a year and a day after this historic decision. The little girl who wanted so badly to learn to read had lived to see the end of school segregation. Because of her dedication, thousands of African Americans had greater opportunities.

Remembering Bethune's Dream

A few years before she died, when Bethune was seventy-eight years old, she wrote, "Our aim must be to create a world of fellowship and justice where no man's skin, color or religion, is held against him." All her life she worked for that goal.

During her life, Bethune received many awards. In 1974 she became the first African American and the first woman to have a monument erected on public parkland in Washington, D.C. Today she is remembered as a dedicated educator and an outstanding leader.

Glossary

discrimination unfair treatment of a person or group, based on race or gender

literate able to read and write

philanthropist a person who gives money to worthwhile causes

poll tax money paid in order to vote

segregated separated from others, especially by race